Uncle Sam Cooks
The Books

by
Andrew M. Gause

SDL Press
Hilton Head Island, S.C.

First Printing 2003

ISBN 0-9656589-3-7

Cover Art
SDL Graphics

Additional copies
available for purchase.
Please send your inquiry to:

Andrew M. Gause
Box 198
Hawthorne, NJ 07507

Phone orders:
800-468-2646

www.SecretWorldofMoney.com

In Loving memory of my brother Leonard J. Gause
1956-2001

"No one pulls the wool over
the eyes of a Gambini"

My Cousin Vinny

With special thanks to:
Fred Dashevsky, Matthew DuHaime, Donna
Thompson, Gina Pontrelli, Dan Polin, DeDee
Gause and Anthony DeLorenzo. Also, a special
thanks to the staff at SDL, without whom this could
not have happened.

Thanks Roger!

Cover concept and execution: Gina and Donna Pontrelli

Another Book by Andrew Gause is
The Secret World of Money
ISBN 0-9656589-0-2

Table of Contents

Introduction

I set out to write this book as a simple easy read that would explain the chicanery revealed in the wake of the Enron Hearings of 2002. It struck me as odd that the Federal Government would be raising such a ruckus over the very acts that they themselves were guilty of. It reminded me of an allusion to the proverb, referring to the so called "Glass house" in Great Britain's St. Martin's Fields, where the Duke of Buckingham lived. The Duke supported attacks against Scotch followers of King James. In fierce retaliation, a crowd smashed windows of his house. A court favorite complained to the King, who replied, "Steenie, Steenie, those who live in glass houses should be careful how they fling stones."

The accounting practices at the nation's biggest U.S. companies may be fraudulent, but their most creative accounting techniques can't hope to rival the financial antics practiced by the world's largest corporation, the United States Government. Exaggerated earnings, disguised liabilities, off-budget expenditures, they are all practiced daily by Uncle Sam on a scale not even the biggest companies could dream of matching. WorldCom Inc. executives brought America's second largest long distance phone company to the brink of bankruptcy, after using improper accounting to pad earnings by $3.8 billion. In 2001, when Congress was faced with a similar need to bolster the bottom line, lawmakers simply voted to shift the date by which corporations had to make a quarterly tax payment. The result was $33 billion in badly needed revenue which the Government accountants simply reported as revenue in the previous quarter. The Federal Government's practices of hiding liabilities are far, far worse than Enron's. When the Savings and Loan Industry debacle occurred, it left a debt approaching $1,000,000,000,000.00 (1 trillion) that the U.S. taxpayer was obligated to pay. Rather than allow this debt to remain on the books, a special corporation was formed. A GSE, called The Resolution Trust Corporation, assumed the entire debt. This RTC was a hopeless corporation with no prospects of ever making money. It never was intended to make money. Hiding the debt so that it was not subject to the debt ceiling, that was its purpose. This enormous debt, left on the Government's books, would reduce the amount which Congress could borrow and spend.

This highlights Uncle Sam's most horrendous accounting practice. They refuse to cap spending. This ongoing exercise piles more liabilities onto an already sky high and some say unpayable National Debt. With this attitude why have a debt ceiling at all?

To avert a Federal default, on June 28, 2002, President Bush signed a bill to increase the public debt limit from $5.95 trillion to $6.4 trillion and this fact was barely mentioned by the mainstream press. Over the years, the GAO has published a long list of documents detailing the auditing sins of various Government agencies. They range from estimates of hundreds of billions of dollars unaccounted for at the Defense Department, one of the worst offenders, to $12.1 billion in improper Medicare payments in 2001. Mainstream media ignored the story. You would think taxpayers would be storming the White

House with picket signs or pitchforks. "Stop spending more than you take in!" Or that the message would be relayed at the ballot box with Congress being turned over in droves. However, for the most part, the public is unaware of this financial chicanery. Most politicians continually misrepresent the true financial condition of the Nation in an effort to remain in office. The last group who stood up for fiscal responsibility was the Congress of 1994. They proposed spending cuts, refused to raise the debt limit, and wanted to scrutinize spending. They shut down Government to make their point. How did we repay them? More than half were voted out of office. No politician wants to publicly admit that we're insolvent. Furthermore, we don't want to hear it. Who wants to know that to keep the lights on in the White House we're going to borrow money that our grandchildren will have to pay back. It is much easier to simply raise the debt ceiling, create more money, spend it in your district and have yourself re-elected. To accuse America's corporations of dishonest bookkeeping practices represents the height of arrogance. Grandma said it was "the pot calling the kettle black." No matter how it is characterized, it smacks of hypocrisy.

I would like to see Congress and the President sign off on the books of the United States, much the same way they now expect America's CEOs to. I doubt this will ever come to pass, for while America's CEOs may understand the nature of money, those in Government apparently do not.

Andrew M. Gause

11/11/2002

Words of Art

"Words of Art" describes the reworking of words to describe something different from the basic meaning which most people understand.

The art referred to is subtle deception. The idea is to change the generally accepted meaning of a word or phrase, so as to convey a meaning other than that which was intended. Lawyers use it often. Lawmakers use it almost exclusively.

When naming a Bill or Resolution, the title assigned often implies something that the bill does not do or the opposite of what it will do. The recently passed Banking Secrecy Act, as an example, did not really live up to its name. The name would imply legislation that provided banking secrecy, something we would all expect. Perhaps on the order of "Don't sell my banking records because that would be a violation of 'The Banking Secrecy Act'. In point of fact, the act removed secrecy from banking. It should have been called "The Banking Anti-Secrecy Act" or the "Banking Transparency Act", to convey the proper meaning. What this legislation really did was to require commercial banks to violate the privacy of their own customers. Bank secrecy means people can hide their wealth from prying eyes. "If they can't sees it, they can't seize it." For its part, Government wants to track every dollar so people and money can be taxed. The Banking Secrecy Act makes one think Congress is legislating bank secrecy while in reality it is being taken away.

These actions have grown to be expected from a Federal Bureaucracy that is as bloated as the current incarnation of the U.S. Government. In the George Orwell classic work, *1984*, he popularized the term, "doublespeak". In his world, Big Brother was omnipotent. He told the citizens the "truth" which usually was a lie. War is peace, hate is love. Big Brother's words meant virtually the opposite of the generally accepted definition. His were words of concealment, words of deception, words of art.

Earmarking is one of the words of art used to describe the way incoming Federal Funds are accounted for. The term "earmark", to most folks means to segregate. If you were to earmark a dollar, you would segregate it from the others. Presumably you earmark it to be spent on a specific purpose. F.I.C.A. taxes would be earmarked for Social Security. Gas taxes would be earmarked for highway construction or repairs. One would expect earmarked funds to be laid aside, not touched, and to be used for the service or project it was intended for. Well, perhaps in the world of common sense that would be true. However, in the world of U.S. Government finance, earmarking virtually assures that money will not be spent on the purpose for which it was collected. "Earmarked" funds are routinely spent on other purposes. Imagine that one dollar comes into a Trust Fund established for airport construction or to save the Wild Swamp Rat. The moment the dollar is received, it is earmarked, that is to say, it is logged in. The money is then loaned to the general fund. The result is called "investment" of the earmarked fund. Now the one dollar is shown as an "earmarked" balance in the Save the Wild Swamp Rat Trust Fund. It is sent to the Treasury. The Treasury then reports that it has received one dollar of revenue. Each account shows a one dollar balance. Like magic, one dollar has becomes two. The common term for this is "double booking". When revenues are double booked at America's corporations, someone goes to jail. When it's done in Government it is called budgeting.

There could certainly be a separate book written about the ways in which words are defined in the Federal Government arena. Something like "Doublespeak for Dumbos". Reading these scribes can be quite monotonous. In using this clever method of doublespeak, "investing" the "surplus" actually means spending the money not currently needed. Taxpayer backed Government debt is "investment". "Earmarking" means spending money on something other than the stated purpose, while pretending that you are holding it for the original purpose. Upon examining the structure of earmarked funds, you will understand why the highway Trust Fund has tens of billions of dollars earmarked for repair and building of roads. Yet the roads are not built or repaired. Tens of billions of dollars are earmarked for runways and airports.

Yet pilots tell us the money isn't being spent to improve the airports and they are quite upset by it. Why not spend the money for the purpose it was collected? The answer is because it has been loaned to the general fund to finance other forms of spending that would not be so popular. If in fact the money was spent on the stated purpose, the subterfuge would be revealed. In reality, a dollar can only be in one place at a time. We would not mind lofty gas taxes if our roads were being fixed. But if we fixed the roads, the laws of physics would cease to apply.

By accounting for the money as "earmarked" and representing it with nonmarketable securities, a dollar can be in two places at once. Furthermore, the real quantity of dollars is masked and their inflationary effects on the economy is never sensed. Oh, not to worry about the funds owed to Social Security and Medicare, says Uncle Sam, we have money earmarked for that purpose. It is "invested". Held in trust, in non-marketable United States Treasury debt. There are, however, no published plans to pay back the money that is supposedly held in Trust. As long as it is not spent or paid back, the ruse remains. When you and I think of the word "trust" we know exactly what it means. To trust someone or to hold something in trust is a clear concept. Apparently the Federal Government has a different definition for this word. One that they are not sharing with us. In this instance the generally accepted meaning of the word is almost too clear. So much so, that the GAO felt compelled to include a footnote in their reports. Here is what they wrote about Uncle Sam's use of the word "Trust":

> *"The Federal budget meaning of the term trust differs significantly from its private sector usage. In the private sector, the beneficiary of a trust owns the income generated by the trust and usually its assets. In contrast, the Federal Government owns the assets and earnings of Federal Trust Funds, and it can raise or lower future Trust Fund collections and payments, or change the purpose for which the collections are used."*

In other words, the opposite of a Trust.

It is my contention that words of art only serve to confuse people. If you do not have the money held in Trust and put aside, do not call the medium a Trust Fund. If you are spending borrowed money, do not call it revenue. If dollars are spent on anything other than their intended purpose, do not call them earmarked funds.

Or to paraphrase Grandpa, "Don't pee on my shoes and tell me it's raining."

The Ultimate Word

In 1894, Congress passed a law, entitled in true word of art:

"An Act to reduce taxation, to provide revenue for the Government, and for other purposes."

Received by the President, on August 15, 1894, it became a law (28 Stat. 509, c. 349).

"...there shall be assessed, levied, collected, and paid annually upon the gains, profits, and income received in the preceding calendar year by every citizen of the United States, whether residing at home or abroad, and every person residing therein, whether said gains, profits, or income be derived from any kind of property, rents, interest, dividends, or salaries, or from any profession, trade, employment, or vocation carried on in the United States or elsewhere, or from any other source whatever, a tax of two per centum on the amount so derived over and above four

thousand dollars, and a like tax shall be levied, collected, and paid annually upon the gains, profits, and income from all property owned and of every business, trade, or profession carried on in the United States ... "

Well, what do you know! The act to reduce taxation, actually was the first attempt at an income tax. George Orwell would be proud. This 2 percent income tax was billed as a way to "soak the rich". Only those who made more than $4000 per year in income were actually affected. To the rest of America, this was an "act to reduce taxation". But of course what else could it be?

The Constitution of the United States recognized two classes of taxes, direct and indirect. It lays down rules by which they can be employed. The rule of apportionment for direct taxes, and the rule of uniformity for duties, imposts, and excises. This graduated tax was apparently unconstitutional because it was not apportioned or equal among the population. Congress was trying to collect a tax which was, and still is, unconstitutional through word of art. The Supreme Court struck down this first Income tax because it was unconstitutional to tax one person more than another. That is what the term apportionment was all about. Collect a dollar from each person, that is okay. But a 15 percent tax on one person's income and a 28 percent tax on another's income, that is not apportioned, so it is unconstitutional. But, the great income tax debate was finally settled in 1913, or was it?

The Sixteenth Amendment to the U.S. Constitution, provided for a tax on incomes:

"The Congress shall have power to lay and collect taxes on incomes, from whatever source derived, without apportionment among the several States, and without regard to any census or enumeration".

Solves that nasty little apportionment issue doesn't it? No, frankly it doesn't. The real word of art had nothing to do with apportionment. The hook was, and still is, what are incomes? Through word of art, we assume income means what comes in, what we earn. I urge every American, to consider carefully, the words lawmakers use. Make sure that you understand their meaning. As repeatedly held by the Supreme Court, the Sixteenth Amendment did not extend the taxing power to new subjects or people. It merely removed the necessity for an apportionment among the states. The United States Constitution has not been amended on this subject. Therefore, money derived from labor did not just become "income" because someone wanted to call it that. This limitation still has an appropriate and important function, and is not to be overridden by Congress or disregarded by the courts. In fact, it is essential to distinguish between what is and what is not 'income', before deciding if you have any. To understand the nature of an Income tax, we require only a clear definition of the term 'income'. The Supreme Court dealt with this subject a century ago. They defined the word income accordingly:

"...the gain derived from capital, from labor or both. Here we have the essential matter:

not a gain accruing to capital; not a growth
or increment of value in the investment; but
a gain, a profit, something of exchangeable
value, proceeding from the property, severed
from the capital, however invested or
employed, and coming in, being 'derived'
that is, received or drawn by the recipient
(the taxpayer) for his separate use, benefit
and disposal- that is income derived from
property. Nothing else answers the
description. "
        Eisner vs. Macomber

The reason I have delved so heavily into
this point, has to do with what I view as the most
prominent word of art used in American law. The
ultimate word of art. That word, dear readers, is
income. What is the basis of an "income tax"?
Nearly every American, when asked, would include
their labor as part of their income. But if income is
the "profit" severed from the labor, then what is
the labor worth? Is not labor for money an even

exchange? Or is your labor worth nothing. Buy something, work on it, sell it and make income. Exchange your labor, which already has value, for money which presumably has an equal value and what have you gained? Nothing. It is an even trade. No gain, no income. Tricky, right? Do you have income? Be careful! In the future every dollar will be dear. The actions of the U.S. Government, in dealing with the income tax, displays for all to see, a classic case of double dealing and double speak. I suggest that this same attitude permeates the account books of the Nation. Redefined words, double counted money, deception, and a relentless urge to spend money are all combined to convince you that only proper and prudent actions are being taken on America's behalf. Be ever mindful for words of art.

Trusty Trust Funds

I have been a very active and vocal critic of the Government's handling of the Trust Funds earmarked for special purposes, such as Social Security, the Highway Trust Fund, The Airport Trust fund and 168 others. In my 1996 book, *The Secret World of Money*, I opined that the Trust funds were lakes of debt, out of sight but destined to flood into the broad money supply. This debt was hidden from public view by the use of what the bureaucrats at the time decided to refer to as "Non-Marketable U.S. Government securities". The more appropriate term is "worthless paper". What good is a security that is "non-marketable"?

Enough questions have been raised to justify a serious look at the subject. Finally some answers are forthcoming in the form of a report from the General Accounting Office or GAO. The report, GAO-01-199SP, clearly confirms that the Federal Government's Trust Fund balances are virtually fictitious, effectively double booked. Having studied this issue at length, rest assured I was not at all surprised by these revelations. This is not a new condition. This numerical trickery has been going on right under our collective noses since at least 1970.

President Lyndon Johnson was the first to open accounting's Pandora's Box. He had sought to appoint a commission as early as 1967 to examine Federal budgeting methods. The Commission had a few meetings, and lo and behold they recommended the combination of all Federal Trust Funds into a single Administrative budget.

Trust Funds had always been accounted for as separate entities. Their funds were never commingled with those in the General Treasury. They were treated as distinct line items. Funds which were collected and earmarked for specific spending were not included in the general budget. They were to be held distinct and separate from all other Government monies.

The concept being put forward was one of a unified Administrative budget. It was billed as a way to get an overall view of the Government's total budgetary picture. Combining all budget accounts would supposedly give us a better overall indication of the Government's borrowing needs. Further, it would be helpful in determining the Government's true fiscal condition. It also helped to draw all of these earmarked funds into the sphere of the "all spending eye".

Previously out of sight, these "earmarked" funds created a massive pool of money that could be drawn upon without affecting the overall health of the economy. These funds were not competing for goods and services because they were being "saved". "Investing" these earmarked funds into Treasury debt would be far more seamless if the money was all put into one big pile.

Although it is presently the largest of the Federal Trust Funds, during much of the early 1960s, the Social Security Trust Fund seldom had surplus funds. Often, it in fact spent more than its income and the general fund was used to subsidize the difference. However, by the late 1960s the fund began taking in more than it spent. President Johnson was preparing his final budget in January 1969. As a lame duck President with so many

failures on his plate, he wanted desperately to
present a balanced budget to the people of the
United States. The Federal Government had
not shown a budget surplus since 1957. Under
President Kennedy and all of his predecessors,
Social Security surpluses were kept separate from
the budget. Overall payroll taxes were kept at just
enough to pay benefits and perhaps build a small
surplus. Occasionally, money was needed from
the general fund, but overall the fund was self
supporting. However, using the Commission's
new unified budget concept, President Johnson
proposed that all surplus funds would be included
in his budget and the Social Security surplus of $3.9
billion was simply counted as revenue in fiscal year
1970. This was enough to balance the budget and
report a $3 billion surplus in the unified budget.
That money obviously needed spending. So, spend it
they did.

In 1974, Congress formalized the process by
passing the Budget Act. It provided that Social
Security's operating surplus or deficit would always
be included in overall budget totals. This made little

difference to the budgets submitted over the next 10 years. Surpluses and deficits in the Trust Fund rarely exceeded 2 billion dollars. However, in 1986, Congress enacted a massive increase in Social Security taxes, which facilitated correspondingly massive surpluses in the Social Security Trust Fund. These surpluses were earmarked and then used to report all subsequent budget positions. So those deficit budgets we remember from the early 1990s, and even the "surpluses as far as the eye can see" which President Bill Clinton promised us, and the "generation of surpluses" House Speaker Newt Gingrich mentioned, all included the ever growing Social Security Trust Fund and these so-called leaders knew it.

Every Administration since Johnson's has used this unified budget as it suits them. To further show their complicity, losing entities are treated differently. Whenever an entity such as the Resolution Trust Corp. or the FDIC threatens to create a deficit position, it is cut from the unified budget immediately. When the unified budget first reported a surplus of nearly $70 billion in 1998, the on-budget accounts were still in deficit by $30 billion. In 1999, the unified budget ran a $124 billion surplus, nearly all of which was the result of the Social Security surplus. From the FY 1996 Budget document entitled: <u>*Analytical Perspectives,*</u> we find this informative tidbit:

> *"Treasury accounts for earmarked monies by crediting these collections to the appropriate funds. Any surpluses resulting from these collections are then lent to the general fund of the Treasury and the funds in most cases are given special, nonmarketable Treasury securities in return."*

In fact, when a payment comes into a Trust Fund account, it can be used for any other purpose as long as an entry is made and the funds are "earmarked". Quoting from the same report, pg. 251:

> *"These balances are available to finance*

future benefit payments and other Trust Fund
expenditures - but only in a bookkeeping
sense. "

A bookkeeping sense indeed! The money is gone the
minute it is sent in. How on earth can this be called
a Trust Fund? If you are holding money in trust for
a specific purpose, you are not supposed to borrow
that money and spend it on something else. In the
private sector, this would be viewed as a breach of
fiduciary responsibility. A crime in many instances.
Why bother to call it a trust at all?

Again from *Analytical Perspectives*:

"Although the special Treasury securities are
non marketable, like other Treasury securities
they are backed by the full faith and credit of
the United States Government. However, if
sufficient surpluses are not available to
redeem the securities, the Government would
either need to increase borrowing from the
public or raise future taxes. "

I love how they refer to these securities as "special". The only thing special about them is that they have no value. The point of putting real money aside is to actually have it when you need it.

Contrary to popular opinion, the baby boomers have been tremendous savers. They are a huge generation and in Social Security taxes alone they have saved $2.3 trillion. In fact, 12.5 percent of every payroll dollar they have received in payroll for the last 15 years or so was supposed to be earmarked for their retirement. The demographics of this generation should not be a surprise to anyone. We are called baby boomers because we are such a large generation. The idea was that this generation would not be a burden on their children. The kids would not need higher taxes to pay for the boomers because they had saved such a huge amount of money. However, irresponsible politicians have borrowed our savings and spent them. The next working generation has very few options. There are not enough workers. In order to repay this money they can either increase borrowing or raise taxes. I left out the choice of

Schematic of Federal Financing
How they spend twice what they take in

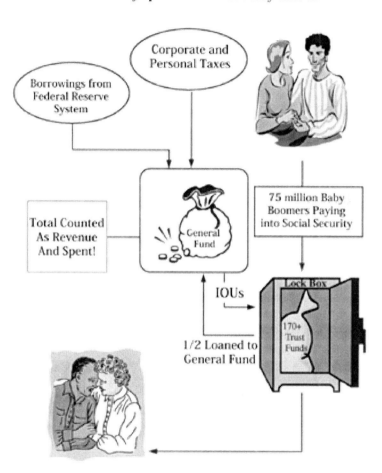

About 1/2 of
collections are used
to pay current retirees
(35 Million People)

cutting benefits because with most of the "Trust
Funds" there is not enough political will to tell
the recipients that we can not pay those benefits.
In fact, most apologists refer back to this Trust
Fund as though it actually had something of value
in it. The existence of these Trust Funds filled with
these "special non-marketable securities" doesn't
change the Government's ability to pay Social
Security benefits. Payments are not increased
when the Trust Fund runs a surplus. They are not
decreased when it runs a deficit. All excess funds
are presumed to be saved for future retirees. But
to the policy wonks in Washington, as long as the
General fund has sufficient money to pay current
Social Security benefits, nothing else matters. They
can borrow all of the surplus, after earmarking it
of course, and spend it to shore up the rest of the
budget. Again from *Analytical Perspectives*:

> *"The vast majority of earmarked funds take*
> *in more than their current needs. On an*
> *annual basis, this is often described as having*
> *a 'surplus'. The accumulated surpluses result*

in these funds having a 'balance'. The balances of earmarked funds are assets of the funds in that they provide a claim on the general fund of the Treasury for future spending. However, the balances are not cash. As with all other money collected by the Government, the general fund of the Treasury receives the actual earmarked taxes and fees paid by the public. Treasury then credits these collections as assets (often in the form of Treasury securities) to the appropriate fund accounts. From the general fund's perspective, these fund assets are a liability."

You better believe it's a liability, a huge liability at that. This, my friends, is double speak at its finest. The "Lock Box" method that candidate Al Gore emphasized during his failed Presidential campaign, is only a variation on this theme. The real quandary to this savings method is that spending for Social Security is already rising sharply as a result of the retirement of the early stage baby boomers. As we will explore further on, large budget deficits will reemerge, requiring more cash than the Fund is taking in.

How ludicrous is this whole arrangement? Can you imagine getting your paycheck, cashing it, then depositing the entire amount of cash into a "Lock Box". This box is now your retirement savings. To fund your ordinary household expenses, you borrow whatever you need from the box. As you use the cash, you deposit IOUs in the Lock Box. Now you can save your entire pay for retirement and meet all of your household expenses. Is this magic? No, that is the magical process called "investing the surplus" that we employ in Washington. Although these surplus monies may be "earmarked" for future retirees, they will still be "invested" and spent as part of the general fund. The real hook here is that these amounts must be repaid before they can be spent on the stated purpose. Think about your lock box. Although it may appear to others that you will have a comfortable retirement based on the amount of "assets" in the lock box, you know these are merely

your own IOUs. You can not retire until they are
repaid. We may be able to put off fixing the roads
and airports. We may also put off the repayment
of other Trust Funds. But retirement, that comes
as sure as the passage of time. Occasionally we
glimpse an honest appraisal of the situation, usually
accompanied by double talk and stammering.
Consider the recent exchange on the television
program, *Evans and Novak* with special guest,
Senator Thomas Dashle:

*Novak: "Senator, do you believe there is a Social
Security Trust Fund?"*

Daschle: "Ah, yes, I do."

*Novak: "What's in it? Can you tell me what's in
it?"*

*Daschle: "Legally, there is a requirement that that
money be invested, and you could call that a fund,
yes."*

Novak: "But there is no such fund, though?"

Daschle: "No there is no such fund per se. Right now we are using Social Security Trust Funds to pay for other spending in the Federal budget, and that to me... isn't what we should be doing. That money should be held in trust."

This was a rare admission by a sitting member of Congress. Some time earlier, Treasury Secretary Paul O'Neill had expressed similar sentiments. In return for his candor, he received a stinging and public rebuke from Congressman Charles Rangel. Rangel, a member of the Joint Committee on Taxation for the 104th Congress, incredulously asked what could be more real than non-marketable treasury securities? My question for Charles Rangel is, "Do *you* really believe this?"

Indeed, Paul O'Neill found himself defending his remarks to all variety of outraged public representatives in the days that followed. How dare he tell such a bald faced truth. His contention was simple and accurate. There are no marketable securities in the Social Security Trust Fund. Treasury admits as much in the name they have given to these financial instruments. A non-marketable security can not be marketed. In one of his final letters to lawmakers on this subject, O'Neill acknowledged that:

> *"...because the Social Security Trust Fund does not consist of real economic assets, we are left to rely on the Federal Government's future decisions to either raise taxes, reduce spending or increase borrowing from the public..."*

He stood his ground to the end. I guess that was the problem. There is no room for honesty in this equation. Let us kill the messenger. No wonder Paul O'Neill had to go. Do not be dismayed. Maybe he will run for President?

The Great White Father

Although the Trail of Tears is not well known to most Americans, it summarizes the plight of Native Americans in dealing with the U.S. Government. The so called Indian wars were responsible for the forced relocation of Indian tribes into the Western territories. They were given 30 million acres of land as reservations "for as long as the eagle flies". However, by 1877, Westward expansion had reached the Reservations. The U.S. Government decided to sell two thirds to white settlers. The remainder was divided into 100 acre parcels and deeded to individual Indians. The Federal Government said it would hold these lands in trust. On my, there is that word again. Needless to say, somehow the records were misaligned, to put it kindly. In testimony before Congress, the Government has acknowledged that the Trust Fund generates $500 million a year in revenue for oil and mineral development. However, Indians leaders have long complained about a lack of accounting and payments which they viewed as inadequate. In 1996, a $10 billion class action suit was filed on behalf of more than 300,000 American Indians. The trial portrayed a damning picture of the handling of the Trust Funds. Investigators discovered that some money that was owed was never collected. Some that was collected was spent on other purposes. Moreover, a century worth of records was destroyed by the Government. The court was not amused. In an unprecedented move, it held Treasury Secretary Robert Rubin and Interior Secretary Bruce Babbitt in contempt for failing to halt the destruction of these records. U.S. Judge Royce Lamberth said, "I have never seen more egregious misconduct by the Federal Government." Ruling in favor of the Indians in 1999, he ordered the Interior Department to account for the funds and revamp the system of payments to provide a more accurate accounting. The Department of Interior couldn't comply with the Judge's order and simply cut off payments altogether to thousands of recipients. The Bureau Of Indian Affairs' web site blamed the lawsuit for the payment failures. The Government denies of course that this was done in retaliation. In the Fall of 2002 the case was in court again. A new Interior Secretary, Gale Norton, was held in contempt on five counts for failing to repair the problem and for providing the Judge with false reports. The Judge's scathing ruling said "I have never seen such a concerted effort to subvert the truth-seeking function of the judicial process." To date, the Department of the Interior has spent over $600 million. Further, it proposes spending an additional $2.5 billion over the next 10 years to reconstruct the records that were lost. The Indians say they are owed over $100 billion. The Government says they don't know what they owe. Chances are the amount will be hefty. Either way, here is another $100 billion or so that does not appear as a liability on Uncle Sam's cooked books.

Cash or Credit

If you run a business and employ an accountant, then most likely your revenue and expenses are recorded in the period they are incurred. If you make a purchase on credit, the full amount of the debt is entered on your books when it is incurred regardless of when you actually pay it. This is the accounting basis that generally is required to be used in order to conform to generally accepted accounting principles (GAAP) in preparing financial statements.

The Federal Government in its accounting to us, uses the more liberal cash basis of accounting. Any money that comes in whether from taxes due or in borrowed funds, is counted as revenue. Any debts that are immediately payable are counted as expenses or costs. If a debt is not yet due, it is not counted at all. They do not record future debts. They only record the amount actually due and payable in cash in that year. Benefit payments and tax receipts are credited or debited using this Cash method. Payroll taxes are counted as revenue when they are received, but benefits are not counted until they are actually paid. Use of this cash basis accounting generally is not considered to be in conformity with GAAP. Most businesses in America must use the more strident accrual method of accounting. Revenue and expenses must be recorded in the period in which they are earned or incurred regardless of whether cash is received or disbursed in that period. The primary difference in these methods is the timing used in recording the transactions. Cash and accrual methods can produce the same results. The results produced will only be different when a great deal of credit is employed. If all of the revenue the Federal Government collects is considered "income" and only the benefits of the current generation are considered expenses, the magnitude of the situation is cleverly concealed.

At the end of fiscal year 2001, the U.S. Government reported liabilities of $7,384 trillion, compared with $6,856 trillion for September 30, 2000. (Fig 1). The largest component of these liabilities ($3.3608 trillion) is represented by

United States Government Balance Sheets
as of September 30, 2001 and September 30, 2000

(In Billions of Dollars)	2001	2000
Assets:		
Cash and other monetary assets	108.0	104.9
Accounts receivable	34.2	32.3
Loans receivable	208.9	207.6
Taxes receivable	21.1	23.3
Inventories and related property	183.8	185.2
Property, plant and equipment	306.7	298.5
Other Assets	63.4	59.7
Total Assets	926.1	911.5
Liabilities		
Accounts payable	95.7	91.0
Federal debt securities held by the public	3319.8	3409.9
Federal employee and veteran benefits payable	3360.8	2764.7
Environmental and disposal liabilities	306.8	301.2
Benefits due and payable	86.0	77.8
Loan guarantee liabilities	27.7	37.3
Other liabilities	188.1	175.0
Total liabilities	7384.9	6856.9
Commitments and contingencies		
Net position	(6458.8)	(5945.4)
Total liabilities and net position	926.1	911.5

Fig 1

pension, disability, and health care costs for Federal, civilian and military employees, as well as for veterans. Honestly, I believe a larger portion of these liabilities are not included in these figures.

The facts in these pages came to be from material gathered from the GAO reports, Federal budget documents, and Social Security Trustee's reports. I do not rely on the accuracy of these numbers. The GAO apparently has an issue or two with the books as well. Quoting from the summary cover sheet on their budget review:

> *"Our report on the U.S. Government's consolidated financial statements for fiscal years 2001 and 2000 is enclosed. We were unable to express an opinion on the consolidated financial statements because of certain material weaknesses in internal control and accounting and reporting issues which prevented us from being able to provide the Congress and American citizens an opinion as to whether the consolidated financial statements are fairly stated in conformity with U.S. generally accepted accounting principles... "*

I had encountered these disclaimers before in the annual reports of companies like Global Crossing, Enron, WorldCom, Adelphia, and I am sure there were a great many others. However, the more of the Federal Government's documents that I read, the more disclaimers I would find. It seemed even the disclaimers had disclaimers!

> *"Net Position, Statements of Net Cost and Balance Sheets, for the fiscal years ended September 30, 2001 and 2000, we were unable to, and we do not, express an opinion on these consolidated financial statements. Revenue/(Cost) to the Budget Surplus and the Dispositions of the Budget Surplus were not audited by us and, accordingly, we do not express an opinion on them."*

Read this gem of a disclaimer:

> *"As a result of the material deficiencies in the Government's systems, record keeping, documentation, and financial reporting, readers are cautioned that amounts reported in the consolidated financial statements and related notes may not be reliable. Material deficiencies also affect the reliability of*

certain information contained in the accompanying Management's Discussion and Analysis and other financial management information--including information used to manage the Government day to day and budget information reported by agencies-- which is taken from the same data sources as the consolidated financial statements. "

Even the Trustees reports had these statements:

"We have not audited and do not express an opinion on the Stewardship Information and Supplemental or Other Information included in the accompanying fiscal year 2001 Financial Report of the United States Government. The Government did not maintain adequate systems or have sufficient, reliable information to support information reported in the accompanying consolidated financial statements as described below. "

It is not just the money that they can not seem to

account for. Consider the nearly $300 billion listed as physical property. (Fig 1):

"Property, Plant, and Equipment and Inventories and Related Property, the Government could not: satisfactorily determine that all such assets were included in the consolidated financial statements, verify that certain reported assets actually exist, or substantiate the amounts at which they were valued."

Finally, the loan accounting line item of only $37 billion far understates the real liability:

"Loans Receivable and Loan Guarantee Liabilities, for fiscal year 2000, certain Federal credit agencies responsible for significant portions of the Government's lending programs, most notably the Department of Agriculture (USDA), were unable to properly estimate the cost of these

*programs, or estimate the net loan amounts
expected to be collected, in conformity with
U.S. generally accepted accounting principles
and budgeting requirements. "*

It is bad enough that we can not get straight
answers from the Congress. But most people
assume someone is checking the numbers. What a
stunner that the General Accounting Office
expresses doubt about the Government's books.
Add to that, the reality that even those in charge
are ignoring this evidence and the situation
becomes grave indeed. Like any true addict,
Government must recognize that it has a problem.
Only then can true healing begin.

Social Spending

As we move forward we face stark, unforgiving demographic challenges. Thirty million people were born between 1933 and 1941. Those folks are now between 62 and 70 years old. These are not the baby boomers. They are already retired and collecting a portion of the FICA payments made by the seventy-five million babies who were born in the United States from 1946 to 1964. This generation, known as the baby boomers, were a by-product of a pent up post war economy. These children, born to grateful returning servicemen and the women who waited for them, outnumber their parents by better than 2 to 1. By 2008 the first wave of baby boomers become eligible for Social Security benefits. We can not count on more workers because people are having fewer children these days. 30 years ago women in the developed countries were having five children each. Today there are 1.6 births per woman.

At these rates, by 2020, there will be 2 people over age 65 for every teenager. Furthermore, a decrease in birth rates has provided us with an elderly population that already comprises almost 13 percent of the total U.S. population. In 30 years, one in four people will be 65 years of age or older. Today one in seven are over age 65. As recently as 1965 there were twelve children for every person over eighty-five. Within 20 years that number will be one to one. People over 85 will increase in population by six times and the 65 to 84 year old group will triple in size. These retirees also have an expectation of an extended period of good health thanks to recent medical breakthroughs. Life

(Fig. 2) Estimates of Social Security fund solvency	Trustees' Report Estimates as Of 01/01/2002	Financial Report Estimates as Of 01/01/2001
First Year Expenditures Exceed Tax Revenue:		
Social Security (OASI and DI)	2017	2016
Federal Old-Age and Survivors Insurance (OASI)	2018	2016
Federal Disability Insurance (DI)	2009	2008
Federal Hospital Insurance (Medicare Part A)	2016	2016
Year Trust Fund Assets Are Exhausted:		
Social Security	2041	2038
Federal Old-Age and Survivors Insurance	2043	2040
Federal Disability Insurance	2028	2026
Federal Hospital Insurance	2030	2029

expectancy has made a greater gain in the last fifty years than it had in the previous five thousand. Geneticists are starting to understand the genetics of aging. The Rudman Study of Human Growth Hormone, published in 1990, revealed the forefront of longevity research. According to this report, in the second half of this century, people will live 150 years or beyond.

As the percentage of the population over 65 reaches 20 percent in 2035, Federal spending on the elderly will require unsustainable levels of income. As this generation employs technology to live longer and spend more time in retirement, a rapid escalation of Federal spending for Social Security, Medicare, and Medicaid is virtually certain to overwhelm the rest of the Federal budget. In the chart on page 46 (Fig. 2) you will find information regarding the trustees estimates for the Social Security Trust Fund. Frankly, I believe they are way too optimistic.

(Fig 2) The First Year Expenditures Exceed Tax Revenue represents the point at which the Trust Funds would have to start using interest income to make benefit payments. In order to use the interest, the Trust Funds would have to redeem securities. To finance redemption, the Government must raise taxes, increase borrowings from the public or cut spending for other programs.

(Fig 2) The Year Trust Fund Assets Are Exhausted represents the point at which all Trust Fund assets (Treasury securities) have been redeemed. After this date, these respective programs will not have adequate resources to pay promised benefits or obligations in a timely manner.

The Medicare program is in greater financial difficulty than Social Security. The Medicare Trust Fund faces rapidly rising health care costs. How will society pay the costs of health care for a much larger aging population? The Medicare Part A program is facing a long range crisis by 2016. The impending retirement of the baby boomers will exhaust the fund quickly, leading to a curtailment of health care services to beneficiaries or an increase in taxes otherwise known as contributions. The Board of Trustees has urged Congress to address the problems facing the Medicare Part A Trust Fund which helps pay for care in a hospital and skilled nursing facility, home health care and hospice care. Starting in 2010, the baby boomers will have a critical influence on the growth in this program's costs. The Board of Trustees of the Medicare Part B Trust Fund note that program costs have generally grown faster than the GDP and that this trend is expected to continue. The increased costs are easily attributable to the seemingly endless growth in the variety of services Medicare will pay for. Medicare Part B helps pay for doctors, outpatient hospital care and other medical services. Discussions instead, are focused on a new prescription drug benefit. How much will this cost?

The retirement of the baby boomers will also mean more people will be utilizing these varied and expanding services. Medicare Part B is in fact running a deficit right now. Premiums only cover about 25 percent of the actual costs. The only reason Part B survives is because the general fund pays the difference. Medicare Part B expenditures are increasing far faster than Medicare Part A. I doubt there will be a race to see which politician is going to be the first to suggest a cut in these benefits?

However, at some point the line will have to be drawn. By 2030, the entire baby boom generation is over age 65 and receiving Social Security, Medicare, and I am sure, another varied batch of vote-inducing goodies. They are slowing down, their health is declining, their physical and mental ailments are increasing. Heart disease, Parkinson's, Alzheimer's, stroke and other chronic illnesses are sending almost a quarter of them to long term care facilities. The 18-65 year olds of 2030 are a much smaller generation than the current one. They will be struggling to support their aging parents. All Federal taxes they pay are diverted to either interest payments, entitlements, and repayment of the Trust Funds. Leaving nothing for them or their children to feast upon. The resentment will breed contempt that would better be directed at the politicos responsible. Why not deal with them now?

Another wild ingredient to this lovely brew is the projections regarding Immigration. Much to the surprise of the INS and most Americans, the Social Security Administration has projected a 900,000 annual increase in immigration. Each time they move the projected life span of the fund forward, they do so by raising the number of immigrants expected to flood our borders. Yet even with this unwanted influx, there are still too few workers, too little capital, burgeoning debt and a struggling economy. Will this be the end of the world as we know it? I doubt it. I think we can learn from the baby boomers' past, anticipate the future, and take steps to turn it to our advantage.

For starters do not assume that the dollar you save today will be of the same value tomorrow.

Budget Busters

In 1789, Congress assumed the total Revolutionary War debt of $78 million. Since then, Congress has tried several times to set an overall ceiling on the amount of the debt outstanding. In 1946, $275 billion was set as the limit. It remained in effect until 1954. In the past 50 years, Congress has enacted 60 such increases to the debt ceiling. On August 10, 1993, the Congress set the debt limit at $4.9 trillion. Nearly two years later, in October 1995, the limit was reached. However, it wasn't until March 1996, that the ceiling was raised to $5.5 trillion. These six months produced a most delicate soufflé of creative accounting, shifted assets, with a twist of the lip. The actions taken during the intervening periods to meet Federal obligations without exceeding the debt ceiling are mind boggling.

When the Congress reaches its debt limit, either spending must be cut or the limit must be increased. But once they discovered how to remove or "invest" surpluses from the Trust Funds, exponential growth has followed. To date, $2.463 trillion has been removed from Federal Trust Funds such as the Social Security funds, the Civil Service fund, and the G-Fund, which pays retirement benefits for government workers and even a few non-workers. To date, it has not been replaced.

Why was the debt ceiling put there in the first place? If not to act as a buffer against profligate Federal spending. Whatever the intention, it didn't work. Treasury virtually ignored the debt limit, allowing Congress to circumvent the law and make a mockery of sound fiscal policy. How did this happen? More importantly, why were the laws ignored?

Under similar circumstances in 1985, Treasury Secretary James Baker announced that he would sell Treasury Securities in the Social Security Trust Fund to raise cash until Congress increased the debt limit. Congress convened a hearing on the subject in September of that same year called, the "Hearing on Disinvestment of the Social Security Trust Fund to Finance the Public Debt."

Up until that time, when Government wanted to borrow Trust Fund assets, they exchanged fully registered Treasury bonds which were then subject to the debt limit. The recipe Secretary Baker was concocting involved taking all of these bonds out of the Trust Funds, sell them, use the money, and replace the bonds with nonmarketable, unregistered, IOUs. Secretary Baker assured one and all that when the debt limit was raised, the securities would be replaced by buying them back on the open market. Congress bought into the subterfuge and agreed to loot America's retirement funds instead of practicing responsible financial stewardship.

A $4.8 trillion national debt by late October 1995, was comprised of about $3.5 trillion in the form of Treasury securities held by the public and the Federal Reserve Banks. The $1.3 trillion difference was comprised of these nonmarketable Treasury securities. Not only were they never repaid, they were spreading like melted butter. These IOUs were now held by every Federal Trust Fund. In subsection (k) of 5 U.S.C. 8348, Congress

Federal Debt
(In Billions of Dollars)

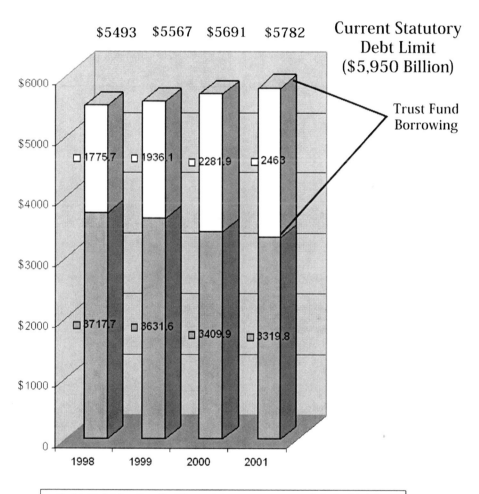

$5493 $5567 $5691 $5782 Current Statutory Debt Limit ($5,950 Billion)

Trust Fund Borrowing

1775.7 1936.1 2281.9 2463

3717.7 3631.6 3409.9 3319.8

$6000
$5000
$4000
$3000
$2000
$1000
0

1998 1999 2000 2001

■ Debt Held by the Public □ Intragovernmental Debt Holdings

authorized the Secretary of the Treasury to redeem any securities held in the Civil Service retirement Trust Fund. As long as the money was used to prevent the amount of public debt from exceeding the debt ceiling. A sneaky way of defeating the ceiling by the amount contained in the fund, about $350 billion at the time. Remember, on a cash basis more money was flowing out in transfer payments and other U.S. obligations, than there were taxes coming in. So all of the excess contributions to Social Security and the other funds still left a gaping hole which Senator Ernest Hollings of South Carolina estimated at about $1 billion a day. In his editorial on the subject, Mr. Hollings noted:

> *"This gimmick is called 'unified budgeting' with a 'unified' deficit or surplus. It's a fraud. With the present surplus fever, the people think the Government is finally on a pay-as-you-go basis. But in reality, the politicians continue to spend, running huge deficits in the Trust Funds."*

During this period Congress further bolstered their subterfuge by enacting Public Law 104-103 which provided Treasury with the authority to issue uncounted securities to meet the March 1996 Social Security payments. *(Which I believe revealed the sorry condition of this, the largest of all Government Trust Funds!)* With all of its supposed surplus, it didn't have enough cash to pay one month's benefit to the current generation. How on earth will they pay the trillions that we now owe? The Federal Government could not redeem any of the debt it owed the fund. Using this magical formulation, they incurred yet another $140 billion in additional debt that would normally have been considered subject to the debt ceiling. Finally, Congress passed Public Law 104-115 which exempted Government Trust Fund investments from the debt ceiling altogether! This master stroke of fiscal magic provided the cushion to allow the politicians to pretend to care about the growing debt, when in reality it was pork chops for all. Even while they were dividing the pie, many on Capitol Hill expressed the need to do the right and responsible things necessary to save

Social Security. Ever the statesman, Senator Ernest
Hollings wryly commented:

*"Obviously, the first way to save Social Security is
to stop looting it.".*

GSEs

Government sponsored enterprises (GSEs) are a
magical combination of Federal agency and
corporation. They appeal to politicians when
cumbersome debt restrictions limit borrowing or
when a profitable activity presents income
possibilities. There are also many politically
attractive reasons for moving these enterprises off
budget. Firstly, debts can be removed from the
budget by transferring them to the GSE as with the
Resolution Trust Corporation. Secondly, when
politicos are motivated to provide patronage jobs
for their cohorts, often civil service regulations
make it difficult in typical Government institutions.
However, these rules do not apply at the versatile
GSE. In this environment, elected officials can
appoint loyalists to boards of directors or have
them hired to work for the GSE. In a typical
Government contract, competitive bidding is
required. "Sunshine Laws" insure that all decisions
are made in daylight with an eye on the public
purse. GSEs are permitted to award contracts on

any basis they choose. Usually the political considerations greatly outweigh the public interest. The GSEs are simply used for achieving political ends. In a private corporation, the board of directors is responsible to shareholders. GSEs however, are run by political appointees who are beholden to those who appointed them. They depend on these master chefs to keep the goodies coming. If board members become confused and concern themselves with public service, they will quickly be replaced. Board members of a GSE are able to direct the business to benefit political supporters. Might as well invite your friends to a tasty barbecue of taxpayers. After all, the board member is not responsible to them, they are the main course. As long as the GSE can generate revenues to cover its operating costs and debt service, nothing else matters. GSEs are used to engage in activities that often generate enormous amounts of revenue relative to the costs, regardless of the value to the public interest. At the State level they are used to construct toll roads and bridges. They decide how the tolls are spent without public scrutiny. If they need to add more costly ingredients, a toll hike will usually cover it. At the Federal level GSEs are employed mainly for financial purposes. The Resolution Trust Corporation, mentioned previously, was set up as a place to park the $850 billion in debt generated by the liquidation of the Savings and Loan industry. The savory morsels that were the assets of these failed institutions were greedily consumed by the early guests at the party. All that remained were the bones and the debt and these could not be left to appear on the Federal books. A GSE does not have to be useful to the community, but it must be useful to the system. The RTC does nothing useful except to hide this enormous debt.

Other GSEs enjoy benefits that are nearly unknown in the private sector. GSEs do not pay taxes or license fees. They are exempt from the red tape that stagnates private business. They ignore local zoning and building ordinances. They are exempt from antitrust laws. Furthermore their deliberations enjoy absolute secrecy. In most instances they are not even subject to a cursory

legislative review. Once established, these GSEs
have great incentive to expand their operations.
This generally serves to increase their income and
influence. After operating expenses have been paid,
the excess revenue in a GSE, is held internally and
may be used by management for any purpose it
deems useful. These expenditures are exempt from
public scrutiny. As the activities of GSEs expand, so
does their need for new bonding issues. Remember,
they have the full faith and credit of the U.S.
Treasury behind them. Clearly, as the chief lenders
of this largess, the nation's commercial bankers
have an interest in seeing these enterprises develop
into a smorgasbord of delicacies. A GSE issues
bonds that are backed by the deep pockets of the
U.S. Treasury. Commercial banks purchase these
bonds in wholesale lots at a steep discount for resale
to private retail investors. Unlike a Government
entity, GSEs may issue the bonds with any bank
they choose regardless of competitive bidding.

The legal profession is also actively engaged
in the GSEs. Legions of attorneys act as "bond
counsels" to these entities. The more they borrow

the higher the underwriting fees. On all contracts let out by a GSE, competitive bidding is not a requirement. Contracts can instead be awarded on the basis of political connections. It is virtually impossible to gauge the total amount of this off budget spending. Many entities do not even compile statistics. Prior to 1960, however, revenue bonds issued by GSEs composed only about 30 per cent of total long term debt in existence. Since 1960, off-budget borrowing has increased to about 69 percent of all debt issued. The GAO report on the subject describes GSEs as:

> *"Government-sponsored enterprises (GSEs) are an unusual amalgam of two familiar institutions: Federal agency and private corporation. As with other Federal agencies - Fannie Mae was a part of the Federal Government for 30 years - Federal rather than state law establishes the enterprises. In addition, they are afforded operating benefits not available to other for-profit enterprises,*

including exemptions from state and local income taxes and from the registration requirements of the Securities and Exchange Commission. However, like private corporations, they are owned by shareholders who are entitled to the after-tax earnings and increases in value of the firm. The executive officers are bound to manage the assets of the enterprise in trust for the benefit of owners, while meeting the responsibilities of the company to the Government under its Federal charter. The major defining characteristic of a GSE, however, is that the Federal Government is perceived to back the obligations of the sponsored enterprise with an implicit guarantee."

Congressional Budget Office. <u>Assessing the Public Costs and Benefits of Fannie Mae and Freddie Mac</u> (Washington, D.C.: Government Printing Office, May 1996)

Federal National Mortgage Association (FNMA) and Government National Mortgage Association (GNMA)

These two are otherwise known as Fannie Mae and Ginnie Mae. They are private corporations with the GSE advantage. The largest, FNMA has become a $4.5 trillion company that pumps cheap money to primary market lenders by paying cash for the mortgages which these companies originate. Once a large quantity has been accumulated, they bundle these mortgages into Mortgage Backed Securities, (MBS), for sale through securities dealers. To aid in their marketing is an implicit Government guarantee that investors will receive principal and interest payments regardless of what happens to the underlying mortgages. This transfers that risk effectively into the Treasury of the United States. According to their own financial records, Fannie Mae's loan volume grew at a compound annual rate of 13.8 percent during the third quarter of 2002. They ended the period at $1.742 trillion. But against this enormous figure, the FNMA allowance for loan losses totaled a mere $812 million as of September 30, 2002. Hardly an adequate reserve for a commercial bank, but this business hybrid is not subject to regulatory scrutiny. Remember, GSEs are the ultimate secret control corporation. They receive favorable treatment and special benefits under charters granted by the Congress. In a May 12, 2000 Moody's press release, the credit rating agency touted that these GSEs had "good financial fundamentals, the strong implied Government support of the enterprises, and the competitive advantages they enjoy as a result of their special status". A special status we would all like to have.

Congress created Fannie Mae in 1938, ostensibly as a vehicle to keep the commercial banks honest. Now that commercial banks had the power to monetize bonds, it was felt that an agency with the GSE advantages could set the benchmark for the commercial bankers to compete against. It would be the mortgage source for the common man. A generation later, in 1968, when no one was alive who remembered why FNMA came in to being, it was "privatized". Today, these mortgaged based GSEs exist to create a pool of money in the secondary market for the commercial banks. These agencies issue the bonds, which are then turned into money or monetized as eligible collateral for Federal Reserve Bank discount loans. These hybrid securities are then eligible for Federal Reserve open-market purchases. They are U.S. Government securities for purposes of the Securities Exchange Act of 1934. Yet, they are exempt from registering under the Securities Act of 1933. If you have followed along the money creation trail with us, you will quickly realize that this capital is then used to buy predefined mortgages from original mortgage lenders. They in turn reinvest that money by making more loans. Is it any wonder interest rates have fallen so low? The rest of the financial markets view these as U.S. Treasury Securities. They are eligible for unlimited investment by national banks and by federally insured thrifts. Investors have become more market savvy, the demand for these securities has greatly enlarged. Many financial institutions even resell these securities to ordinary depositors as safe and secure widow and orphan type investments. Incidentally, these securities do not have to be registered with the Securities and Exchange Commission (SEC). This one regulatory pass alone is easily worth billions. Some estimates suggest this exemption is worth $280 million a year to FNMA. As previously mentioned, these agencies are also exempt from paying state or local income taxes. Can you put a value on that? As any small business person could explain, this is an extraordinary advantage. In 1999, this tax exemption reaped an extra $690 million for these private conglomerates.

The most troubling exemption is that the capital requirements imposed on other financial institutions are routinely ignored in a GSE environment. Commercial Banks are thoroughly scrutinized for sufficient preestablished reserve requirements. The GSEs are exempt from this scrutiny. Far from maintaining adequate reserves, Fannie Mae refers instead to a $2 billion line of credit from the U.S. Treasury Department. This advantage means they can have all the capital they need. Fannie Mae is viewed as too big to fail, even if these credit lines were exhausted. This attitude creates even greater financial risk. This is why Fannie Mae's carelessness threatens taxpayers, not just private stockholders.

Because these agencies are creatures of Government, it should be no surprise that they are sympathetic to the needs of the politically connected. Five of Fannie Mae's eighteen directors serve at the pleasure of the President of the United States. Is it any surprise that former Government officials populate the halls of these Government sponsored enterprises? Consider the case of Franklin Raines, the former director of the Office of Management and Budget in the Clinton Administration. All of the budget surpluses reported by former President Clinton came with support from this man's office. He is the current CEO of FNMA. His compensation package tops $8 million a year. Can you imagine any public servant worth $8 million a year? Vice Chairwoman Jamie Gorelick was a Deputy Attorney General under Janet Reno. During the FBI files scandal in the

Clinton White House, conversations concerning improper requests between the White House and the Justice Department were subjects of hot debate. Jamie Gorelick and Jack Quinn, according to depositions, "...had notice of this information and obviously were communicating back and forth." Ms. Gorelick in her position at Justice was hospitable to Jack Quinn and President Clinton's White House. Ms. Gorelick now has a job at FNMA. She made over $2 million in her first year on the job. Not bad for a person with no previous experience in housing finance. Vice President at FNMA, John Buckley was press secretary for Congressman Jack Kemp (R-N.Y.). Vice President Duane Duncan was staff director for Congressman Richard Baker, the Louisiana Republican who chairs the House subcommittee that monitors them. What a convenient arrangement. Lest you figure it's a one way street, occasionally things go the other way. For example, Fannie Mae has almost two dozen flashy law firms on retainer to help spend $4 million a year lobbying Congress. The director of the Congressional Budget Office, Dan

Crippen, was a former Fannie Mae lobbyist. Under his tenure, the supposedly independent Congressional Budget Office did an analysis of President Clinton's budget proposals. In these projections it was assumed that the stock market would yield an average real rate of return of 7 percent annually. Many prominent economists assailed these projections, suggesting that a 3 percent rate would have been a far more plausible assumption. One hand does wash the other. Using the optimistic assumptions provided by the stalwart Mr. Crippen, the books were cooked projecting balanced budgets and a generation of surpluses. These surpluses have of course, vanished, being replaced by deficits as far as the eye can see. The 2003 deficit will exceed $350 billion and the 3 percent real rate of return in the stock market is a distant memory.

Meanwhile, these entities have multiplied their debt by 600 percent since 1992, from $196 billion to nearly $1.5 trillion as of the third quarter of 2002. Yet despite their stated goal of providing a source of mortgage funds for low to moderate income families, these agencies are purchasing fewer loans than the private mortgage market as a whole. The lawyers at Housing and Urban Development have proposed regulations that would require FNMA to increase their commitment to lower income borrowers. The evidence reveals that these "public service agencies" are buying instead, mortgages that were issued to the middle and upper class borrowers. These mortgages would willingly be bought by any secondary market investors. The benefits Fannie Mae and other GSEs collect from indirect Government subsidies go primarily to their top executives and stockholders, not to the lower income mortgage seeking public and certainly not to benefit the taxpayer.

These agencies are anxious to grow into businesses that are not authorized by their charters. Fannie Mae wants to provide life insurance for its borrowers. They have invested in providing automated underwriting services to lenders. Because of their Government sponsored advantages, they can offer these services at prices way below the actual cost of providing them. The risks of failure would fall on the taxpayer. In an effort to counter these charges, FNMA has begun to advertise their intention to purchase more lower income mortgages that have a higher default risk.

Ultimately, FNMA and other GSEs will end up with a large portfolio of risky loans combined with insufficient capital, a recipe for financial disaster. None of these liabilities are included in the Government's budget or debt reporting formulas. A general downturn in economic conditions could send these institutions into insolvency. Fannie Mae will inevitably follow the path of the Savings and Loan bailout. Like the S&Ls, they use short term debt to buy long term mortgages. If the cost of short term borrowing rises, these agencies will quickly be swamped.

If history is any indication, investors will continue to lend money in the belief that the Federal Government will step in to protect Fannie Mae. This is precisely the scenario observed during the S&L crisis. S&Ls lost money due to abnormally high interest rates, but they were kept alive by Federal deposit insurance. Rather than closing, as a private business might do, the S&Ls took on greater risk in order to increase returns, using insured depositors' money.

A 1990 report by the Congressional Research Service stated, *"Deposit insurance meant that depositors had nothing to lose as a consequence of risky lending by thrifts. S&L owners had nothing else to lose as a result of risky lending either. This left the Federal Government as the only party involved that had anything to lose as a consequence of risky lending by the thrifts."* Wow, did we lose.

Furthermore, it seems we never learned the $850 billion lesson that the Savings and Loan crisis should have taught us. Following the same formula, Fannie Mae is becoming the largest issuer of debt in the country. They intend for their debt to replace U. S. Treasury Bonds as the nation's benchmark because they have the ability to issue "unlimited quantities". The end result is a $1 trillion liability that is nowhere included in the Federal calculations of the National debt. These GSEs represent a much larger claim on the Public Treasury than all of the S&Ls did!

The Federal Deposit Insurance Corporation

The FDIC provides deposit insurance to the nation's Commercial Banks and Thrifts. Enacted during a banking crisis, the Federal Deposit Insurance Corporation Improvement Act of 1991 created a mandatory Government managed system. It is funded in part by premiums paid by commercial banks, and in part by a line of credit provided by the U.S. Treasury. The balance is guaranteed by the U.S. Taxpayer.

A deposit insurance system that purports to protect small savers is antithetical to the long term health of the monetary system. Certainly if banks want to band together and sponsor some sort of market based insurance to provide security to the depositor, that is within their purview. However, to expect the taxpayer to accept this risk is a blatant extension of an economic benefit to a select few. Having said that, let us examine the overall condition of this losing entity and others like it.

The liabilities of the Federal Deposit Insurance Corp. (FDIC) should be privatized. It is

one of the examples of a losing entity that has been
cut loose from the constraints of the Federal
budget. The American taxpayers would be better
served if banks themselves assumed responsibility
for underwriting deposit insurance. FDIC liabilities
are seemingly endless. Far too big to fail is a
mentality that permeates the banking industry.
Market discipline, not implied taxpayer's
guarantees, should serve as the protector of
deposits. Market discipline would assure that a
bailout on the magnitude of the Savings and Loan
system would never again be borne by the Public
Treasury. There was an S&L crisis only because
investors were assured that the full faith and credit
of the United States would protect their deposits.
Depositors should be at risk whenever they deposit
money in a bank. They expect similar risk when
investing in bonds or stocks. Why should CDs or
similar bank paper carry any less risk? The total
obligation represented by FDIC insurance is to
cover almost $4.5 trillion deposited in Commercial
Banks and $950 billion in other Savings
Institutions. While perhaps it is doubtful that all

loans would all go bad at once, liabilities at problem banks have roughly doubled over the last year, reaching $37 billion in 2002. Premiums paid in by member institutions amount to only about 1 percent of the total FDIC liability. So, the good news is that we are only obligated for 99 percent or about $4.5 trillion.

National Credit Union Administration Central Liquidity Facility

Public Law 95-630 (November 10, 1978) enacted Title III, the Central Liquidity Facility (CLF). The CLF is another Government Service Enterprise created to improve the general financial stability of credit unions by serving as a liquidity lender to those institutions experiencing unusual or unexpected liquidity shortfalls. Member credit unions own the CLF which exists within the National Credit Union Administration. The President of the CLF manages the facility under the oversight of the National Credit Union

Administration Board. It meets the liquidity needs of credit unions with an implicit loan guarantee. The problem here is the same as the Savings and Loan. These institutions have taken their member's money on short term loans and have lent the money out for long term mortgages. Next time interest rates rise, this facility will be tapped. Who knows how many tens or hundreds of billions this will ultimately cost. Either of these two deposit insurance facilities could present the next dish of smoked taxpayer.

The Export Import Bank

The Export-Import Bank was chartered to provide loan guarantees, insurance, and loans to the nation's exporters when private banks decline. Proponents of the Bank suggest that the program provides a net economic gain by boosting U.S. Exports. That may be so, however only 2 percent of exports are financed by the Bank. The taxpayer's exposure is magnified because the Bank provides its services in areas with excessive political or commercial risk. While under normal circumstances you are not likely to be struck by lightning, if you spend every stormy day standing in a Kansas cornfield, holding an iron rod over your head, your odds rise dramatically. Almost half of this Bank's activities are conducted with so-called emerging economies. Markets that private, unsubsidized entities would not touch because of an investment environment that does nothing to attract foreign capital. In early 1984, Vice President George Bush contacted the Export Import Bank to press fellow Yale graduate, and chairman William

Draper to approve a U.S. backed loan guarantee to Saddam Hussein. Draper explained that no sane banker would loan money to Iraq, but the Vice President persisted. Although the $200 million program was approved, it was suspended in March 1986, when Iraq, surprise, failed to make the payments. By early 1987, Iraq needed money once again. The chief paid lobbyist for this effort was the ubiquitous Clark Clifford, Counsel to every Democratic President since Truman.

Banca Nazionale del Lavoro, BNL, the Italian bank, had an Atlanta, Georgia branch. This bank, with the encouragement of the Administration, was more than willing to loan money, provided it had loan guarantees from Eximbank or Commodity Credit Corporation. At the end of February 1987, Vice President George Bush, once again asked the chairman of Eximbank to assist Iraq. Bush also helped to secure some U.S. export licenses that would allow Saddam to buy very sensitive American technology. BNL managed to process $47 million of Eximbank-backed loans for Iraq. By the end of the 1980s, Washington had approved a total of $5 billion of loan guarantees for Iraq. Assistant Secretary of State Richard Murphy, encouraged Administration officials to believe that assisting Iraq was in the best interest of the United States. Of course it was not. The loans went bad and have never been repaid. Perhaps when the regime changes in Iraq the situation will be reviewed.

Under the Federal Credit Reform Act of 1980, Ex-Im is required to set aside reserves for these potential losses. The reserves have now reached $10 billion. However, the Ex-Im bank faces losses of $75 billion. No one is even discussing, let alone addressing the problem. In fact, the second President Bush has presented a budget which calls for a 25 percent cut in these appropriations. It seems that the Bank generates net losses on operations nearly every year. These losses come in the form of increases in the provision for off balance sheet losses. These losses are not even declared in Export-Import Bank's statement of financial position! The collection of these loans is doubtful. Most at risk are loans in countries such as China and Mexico. Ex-imbank authorized more loans, guarantees, and insurance for exports to China and Mexico than any other countries. The Bank approves loans when the world's wealthiest corporations are not willing to commit their own resources. What does that reveal about the soundness of their activities? Ex-Im Bank's loans and guarantees to Gazprom, the Russian gas monopoly, speaks volumes to the real motivations behind these loans. That is, one of supporting U.S. diplomacy. The real question is at what cost diplomacy. Annually, Congress throws about a billion dollars at the Bank to cover potential losses. The majority of these loans were for products produced by America's corporate giants, like Boeing, Northrop Grumman, General Electric, Lucent Technologies, Westinghouse, and General Motors. Thanks to these policies, U.S. taxpayers face tens of billions of dollars in losses on defaulted loans. This liability is not included in the Federal Budget.

Pension Benefit Guaranty Corporation

Their job is a simple one; to administer pension plans, collect premiums, and make benefit payments to eligible participants whose pension plans terminate without sufficient assets to pay all promised benefits. Under-funded pensions are a serious side effect of the corporate slaughter which began in 2002. Major problems affecting hundreds of thousands of pensions at companies such as Enron, Global Crossing, Lucent, Bethlehem Steel, Adelphia and WorldCom, started to cause real consternation among those who watch the world of money. The problem however, is not limited to these defeated corporations. In reality it's the entire private pension system that is on shaky ground. Bethlehem Steel, for example, has an unfunded pension liability of $5 billion dollars. The stalwart GM has a pension fund that's light by $8 billion. Yet private pension plans are counted on by half of the current work force. Many do not believe that Social Security will be adequate to provide for their retirement. What they are shockingly discovering is that there may be no private pensions either. Many companies either didn't put in the necessary funds or borrowed the money and spent it on something else. Sounds familiar doesn't it? In 1964, the staid automaker, Studebaker, went into an abrupt, messy bankruptcy. Not, however, before draining their pension fund. This left a great many loyal employees holding the bag.

Politicians saw a way to improve their own standing by doling out some treats. A decade later, in 1974, the Employment Retirement Income Security Act (ERISA) was passed by a most generous, vote-seeking, Congress. The act provided for an established prudent practice concerning pension benefits. As part of the act, The Pension Benefit Guaranty Corporation, PBGC, was chartered to deal with corporate bankruptcies as it related to these pension funds. This corporation, and ultimately the taxpayer, would guarantee to pay worker benefits in the event of a shortfall.

In 1978, the 401(k) was added as a vehicle for nearly all companies to provide tax free savings for their workers, and provide they did. By 1990 nearly

20 million people had these pensions. By 2000 the number of participants had risen to 42 million. These pension plans were controlled and invested by the companies instead of the workers. Excess gains were kept by the corporations, without increasing benefits. In the go-go 1980s, American companies took nearly 25 billion "excess" dollars out of their pension plans. They reported these gains as part of their profits. By 2000, with the stock market raging, nearly a quarter of a trillion dollars in pension fund surpluses were reported in this fashion. Many states and larger corporations did not bother to make any deposits into their pension plans. Neither did most government entities. States, municipal governments and political subdivisions of all character rarely bothered with pension deposits during the roaring years. After all, rising stock prices more than provided for benefits, and everyone knew the bull market would run forever. Hindsight is indeed 20/20. Maybe it's unfair to suggest that they should have seen this coming. How about another plate of bankruptcies with a side order of nearly $1 trillion in debt?

The International Monetary Fund

The IMF is best known to the American public as the agency that sent billions of dollars into the financial system during the debt crisis of the 80s, and for the huge amounts given to Mexico and Russia during the 90s. Does anyone consider where this money comes from?

During 1983 and 1984, the IMF lent $28 billion to countries having difficulty meeting their financial obligations. In 1995, it loaned to Mexico over $18 billion. From 1992 through 1996, the IMF provided $20 billion to the Russians. The most telling segment of these maneuvers is where the money went. That's what the lawyers teach us; follow the money. If you do this, you will find that following a brief stay in the target countries, the lion's share of it wound up in the accounts of Goldman-Sachs, J.P Morgan, and other New York banks, who incidentally, are the primary owners of the New York Federal Reserve Bank. How could this happen? The scenario is well played. First, these banks go where no sane banker would, and in

exercises of statecraft, they make loans to
whichever dictator is in power at the time or
whichever one is preferred. They are quite
comfortable that the money will be returned
eventually. After massive currency fluctuations
wrack a nation's economy, the IMF makes loans to
repay these amounts. The IMF says it has no say
over how the money is spent. This is not the case.
In fact the entire approach requires the IMF to be
deeply involved with members' economic policies as
they influence their money's exchange value. The
IMF looks beyond currency value and examines
parts of an economy that influence the exchange
value and to evaluate performance. The present
system demands greater "transparency" and
permits more reasons for the IMF to monitor
national policy. The IMF calls this activity
"surveillance" over members' exchange policies.
If the IMF is able to control the collective nations'
economic policies, then this will lead to stable
exchange rates within a set inflationary policy.
Theoretically, if all nations follow a set recipe, then
there will not be severe currency fluctuations

between nations. If any major country deviates from a set inflationary recipe its currency will quickly reveal the camouflaged worldwide devaluation of money and spoil the party for everyone. Each year IMF staff travels to a members' capital and spends two weeks holding discussions with officials. The mission is devoted to collecting data on employment, interest rates, money supply, exports and imports, wages, taxes, expenditures, and other items of economic interest in that country. The information is then used to determine which actions and policies have been successful during the previous year and which directives or recommendations were ignored. The IMF stands ready to require any number of restrictions on a members' ability to exchange its own currency. After joining the IMF, every aspect of a nation's economic information is transparent. Each country is responsible for passing the necessary laws and for requiring the supplying of information about economic activity. Annually, a report containing "suggestions" about how to address economic weakness is sent to the member's

Government. In reality, this information is used by all manner of speculator to enrich themselves at the expense of the country providing the data. One can see the value of this report, especially to currency raiders and other induced predators. Besides these "suggestions", the IMF holds consultations with the countries whose policies have an influence on the world economy. These meetings review the economic situation. The IMF publishes these reviews twice a year in its *World Economic Outlook*. This publication allows countries to coordinate their own economic policies with other countries. If all members inflate or deflate their currencies in unison, the effects can be more easily hidden from the masses.

Borrowing large amounts of money has also changed the nature of the IMF, making it more like a bank, an unregulated bank, free to influence the world's direction without the impediment of personal rights. Emerging countries are induced by the bankers and their economists to spend more than they take in, making up the difference by borrowing, until their credit is exhausted. That is when the IMF steps in, supplying the country with the foreign exchange necessary to extend its economic life. This is in direct opposition to what the free market demands. A debtor country must demonstrate how it intends to correct its economic problems. The IMF restricts growth or forces increased taxes as a provision to the loans. This type of social engineering is exactly the activity that the IMF claims it is not involved in. In a bow to those who started the spiral, the IMF lends only on the condition that the debtor use the borrowed money to repay the private loans made by the original bankers. Although the IMF was founded primarily to oversee the monetary system from behind the scenes, it occasionally takes direct action and injects huge sums of money through loans to its members. Its financial functions are a significant activity. In fact, these manipulations known as a "dirty float" are exactly what is required to influence currency values when "suggestions" don't work. Annual membership fees constitute the biggest source of money to the IMF. Member countries pay 3/4 of their dues in their own

currency from taxes collected. You know who the
biggest contributor is? The U.S. Taxpayer of
course. Drawing money in this fashion serves two
purposes, the first is that it reduces the amount of
money available in the member nation, thereby
reducing inflation and secondly it provides the
capital necessary for the IMF to conduct its
monetary manipulations. However, almost half of
the money on the IMF balance sheets can not even
be used because they have piled it into gold. To
provide access to a comparable pool of money, the
IMF has a line of credit totaling $25 billion with a
number of Governments and banks throughout the
world. This line of credit, called the General
Arrangements to Borrow, is renewed every five
years. The IMF also borrows money from member
Governments or from their monetary authorities.
Over the past three decades, the IMF has used this
borrowing to provide members with more money
for longer periods and under better terms than they
could obtain on their own.

The influence of this borrowing and lending
on the free market forces that would otherwise

reveal the discrepancies has been astounding. The IMF increases their control with every loan. Although conventional wisdom holds that gold is a barbarous relic, it is still a critical asset in the holdings of the IMF. The restrictions placed on the IMF at its founding, highlighted the role of gold in the international monetary system. The Second Amendment to its charter contained a number of provisions that were intended to achieve a gradual reduction of the role of gold in the international monetary system and allow its accumulation in the IMF. In fact, the IMF has one of the largest official holdings of gold in the world. The IMF holds about 3,217,341 kilograms of gold (103.4 million fine ounces) at designated depositories. What does the IMF have to say about all of this?

> *.... While gold is reflected as an asset in the IMF's balance sheet, it is not used in the Fund's operations and transactions. "*

In this way they can pile up gold while constantly asking for more money. According to Article V, Section 12 (b) of the IMF's Articles of Agreement, any transactions in gold by the IMF requires an 85 percent majority of the total voting power of the IMF. The IMF may sell gold outright on the basis of prevailing market prices. It may accept gold in the discharge of a member's obligations to the IMF. The IMF does not have the authority to engage in any other gold transactions, e.g., loans, leases, swaps, or use of gold as collateral, and the IMF does not have the authority to buy gold. The Amendment also abolished the official price of gold and abolished the obligation to use gold in transactions between the IMF and its members. The Second Amendment required the Fund, in its dealings in gold, to avoid a fixed price of gold, because that would also reveal currency discrepancies. Under the Amendment, members agreed to cooperate with the IMF and other members, with respect to these reserves to permit better surveillance of international liquidity. In 1995, the IMF's Executive Board reviewed the role of gold in the IMF and concluded that the policy on gold should be governed by the following principles:

"As an undervalued asset held by the IMF,
gold provides strength to its balance sheet.
Any mobilization of the IMF's gold should
avoid weakening its overall position. "

More recently, the IMF structured a $41.5 billion international bailout, designed to protect Brazil's currency. The U.S. share is $18 billion ($600 is your share!) What a waste of time and money, and do you know what is going to happen? The money will last long enough to get the "big boys" out. They will sell and receive payment in full. Then Brazil's currency will be allowed to falter. Haven't we seen this movie before? The point that allows such a bailout, is the idea that a Brazilian devaluation may start a global financial meltdown? I think the real intent is to lull us all to sleep and regain investor confidence. This may prevent a descent into Asian-style chaos. If it is the will of the markets, Brazil's currency should be allowed to fall. The investors who put their money there should lose it, but instead we will bail them out. The "hot shots" will take their money and run and then the currency will be allowed to collapse. Who will suffer? Why, the Brazilian people of course. Especially the working class. Boy, does this sound familiar. The fact of the matter is that the Brazilian *Real* is overvalued. If we really want to help them, then let it go now. If a devaluation would be allowed now, those responsible would bear the brunt of the losses. Brazil's exporters would become more competitive and their interest rates would fall. The pain would be spread to those who benefited the most. After all, Brazil should be able to manage a controlled devaluation.

Sooner or later the other shoe has to fall. We can not continue to support the banker's follies throughout the world. The U.S. economy is operating on a consumption driven boom. Asia's problems are far from over, and elsewhere, in Latin America, the concerns about who could be next, have created the ingredients for a global taxpayer barbecue. If one examines the track record of countries involved with the IMF, it will soon become apparent that most are now worse off economically than before accepting the IMF's "help". Sure we have faced this before and survived, but at what cost? A heavy rate of taxation and deficits that just won't quit. Whether or not a disaster can be avoided will depend primarily on whether or not markets maintain their faith that America's Treasury will come to the rescue. I certainly do not see that perception changing. We seem to be more than willing to clean up the losses created by our privately owned banking system. How about we share in the profits? This will be just one more failure in a run of IMF farces. Any attempt to prop up a country with high interest rates and big loans have failed. In fact, if the IMF fails again, they should never be given another American dime. Instead, you can count on at least $10 billion a year going into this cookout.

The Federal Reserve

The ultimate GSE is the one established in 1913 to issue the nation's money. Although it is true that the Bureau of Engraving and Printing prints the notes, it only has one customer, The Federal Reserve Banks. They have been given the monopoly power to create the nation's money and then loan it into circulation. Creating money is not very expensive. With 92 percent of all money being electronically created, the cost of production is very small. Each piece of currency, regardless of face value, has a cost of just 2.5 cents. Electronic money has a cost of a fraction of a cent. Billions of dollars are created at a cost of nearly nothing. The "profit" is used in the general operations of this GSE, once again without the scrutiny of the taxpayer. Spending is brisk, although we are not allowed to see the financial transactions involving the bonds of other nations or the currency swaps. This is where the real cooking goes on. Dollars are printed or electronically created and traded for things like Russian *rubles* or Argentine *pesos*. These items are then counted as assets. Really it is nothing more than covert foreign aid. They do however, show us the day to day spending on more mundane items. So let us marvel at these.

Construction, for example, is a booming business at the Federal Reserve, and it's all done on the whims of the board. Consider the new Federal Reserve Bank headquarters in Minneapolis. It sits on nine acres of riverfront, with a 10-story stone clock tower overlooking terraces and gardens. It offers "James Bond" style security with automated vaults, pistol range, fitness center and subsidized dining. The $108 million Dallas Fed, and a $178 million Atlanta Fed, are buildings constructed in similar style. The Fed is clearly living large and why not? The Fed's inclination is to put its own comfort and prosperity ahead of those it is supposed to serve. The Fed is not shy about constructing these spectacular edifices. These buildings suggest an opulence that Fed spokesmen claim is necessary to reinforce worldwide confidence in the U.S. Banking system. Confidence is an important factor.

The 12 Federal Reserve Banks each operate

with complete independence, and with $475 billion in assets, there is plenty left over despite their spending. The Fed has 25,000 well paid employees. It practically runs its own air fleet comprised of 47 Lear jets and small cargo planes. It has similar fleets of more traditional vehicles, including luxury personal cars complete with drivers. A full-time curator watches a spectacular collection of paintings, sculpture and other works of art. Yet this spending receives no public scrutiny. The Fed funds itself on the interest it collects from the American taxpayer on its gigantic trove of U.S. Government securities, all of them the marketable type, I might add. That is what the Fed demands whenever it creates money for Congress. Every dollar that the Fed wastes on benefits, opulent construction, or overpriced art is a dollar that could have been used to cut the budget deficit. But there is little incentive to do so.

The truth is that the Federal Reserve Banks are very privileged, privately held corporations. Deeply rooted and wealthy, they make their own decisions. The Federal Reserve Banks pay no income taxes. Accordingly, the IRS has no jurisdiction over their financial dealings, which are by law, exempt from audit and oversight. Without such oversight, the Federal Reserve Banks have delved into statecraft, by buying foreign bank paper with U.S. dollars, thereby providing taxpayer funded foreign aid. Without the need to seek normal Congressional budgetary approval for their expenditures, the Fed has quietly amassed a fortune. They admit to taking over $2 billion from citizens annually to fund day to day operations and periodic purchases of expensive antiques and fine artwork. They sponsor chamber music recitals in their lobbies. Their furniture alone is valued at $800 million. Obviously they are not shopping at K-Mart.

The basic structure of the Federal Reserve System has changed little since it was created in 1913. At the turn of the century, Federal Reserve Banks were sited according to politics of the day and the principle that a commercial banker should be able to reach a branch within one day's train ride, in case he needed cash for unexpected withdrawals. Today, these locations make little sense. Missouri, which was once an economic powerhouse because of its Mississippi River and railroading connections, has two Federal Reserve Banks. While a newly populated state such as Florida does not have any. California has a massive economy, yet it shares the Federal Reserve Bank of San Francisco with eight neighboring states. In fact this one bank is responsible for the monetary needs of almost one quarter of the U.S. population. All of these functions could be accommodated by a Treasury owned entity.

What is financially significant is that each of the 12 privately owned Federal Reserve Banks maintains two capital accounts. A paid in capital account and a surplus account. The paid in capital account represents contributions by member banks of the Federal Reserve System. The amount involved equals 6 percent of a member bank's capital. The capital surplus account is funded from the Federal Reserve Banks' earnings after expenses and dividends are paid. In 2001, the value of the capital surplus account was just over 1 percent of the total assets of the 12 Banks. Unlike most other Government sponsored enterprises, the Federal Reserve has not had an annual operating loss since 1915. It makes money every single year. As outlined in the *Secret World of Money*, $280 billion in U. S. currency was held overseas. That is just the currency component. Hundreds of billions in Electronic Dollars are also held in accounts around the world for the purchase of oil. All of these "dollars" are created by the Federal Reserve Banks. The total amount of Federal Reserve notes outstanding was $611.8 billion as of December 31, 2001. The total Electronic volume they have created exceeds $8 trillion. What did these bankers put up for this privilege? As of September 4, 2002, the paid in capital was $8.2 billion. A paltry sum compared to the benefits received. Maybe we can all buy in. Let the Congress print up $8.2 Billion and buy these shareholders out. The capital surplus account was $7.3 billion as of December 31, 2001. Take that money back! Federal Reserve Board officials have suggested publicly that they do not need capital to absorb losses. That is because unlike any other entity, these banks can issue all the money they need. In other words a bank with the power to create money does not need to hold capital. The notion of solvency evaporates when you are the source of money. Technically, losses could make one of these banks insolvent, but all they have to do is create enough money to buy their way out of any problem. So transfer that surplus money to the Treasury. The difference between the surplus and the paid in capital is less than $1 billion. The Federal Reserve System's holdings, including the capital surplus account, could reduce the obligations of the U.S. Taxpayer. Eliminating the capital surplus account and transferring assets directly to the Treasury would cause the Reserve Banks to eliminate Treasury securities from their portfolio, thereby reducing the total U.S. debt. Why do we need a middle man here? We know how to print money.

The Fed continues to issue money to its own advantage. It has sponsored an issue of money that is unprecedented in U.S. monetary history. One can easily calculate the total money issue outstanding.

The more dollars that are made, the less they are worth. What is a dollar? Now we get to the very essence of the problem. We don't know what a dollar is. How on earth are we supposed to make any realistic projections when we don't even know what value the dollar will have at some future point. It's a classic case of Orwellian Style "double think".

Inflation is dead - Long live Inflation!! Haven't we heard enough of this inane, nonsensical talk? The only measure of the dollar that the mainstream media focuses on is the controversial "CPI" or Consumer Price Index. It is a strange work of fiction, indeed. Our Federal Government's yardstick for measuring what life costs is so flawed and incomplete that any meaning attached to the term inflation has been long lost. The CPI excludes so-called "volatile" elements, such as food and energy prices. This, by itself, renders the index almost meaningless. However, the greater absurdity lies in the fact that the Federal Government regularly replaces any vital component of the CPI which has sharply increased in price. A surrogate item of lesser quality or value is substituted. For example, how can we assume that all consumers of increasingly pricey seafood will suddenly develop a taste for tofu, hamburger or ground pork? Moreover, the CPI expressly excludes all taxes which are not directly associated with the purchase of consumer goods or services. Increases in Social Security taxes, which are insidious escalations affecting virtually all wage earners, are not even reckoned into the equation! In addition, property tax hikes, obviously causing an increase in the cost of living, are not even factored into the figures reported.

Our Bureau of Labor Statistics' methodology is oddly arcane and difficult for the average American to understand or follow. I believe this is deliberately done. This index is a hopelessly incomplete measure of the systematic debasement in the value of our dollar. Pretending that the American people can always "substitute" a suddenly expensive item (i.e. home energy costs per kilowatt-hour) with additional insulation or lowering of thermostats is ludicrous. We do not live

Growth In Federal Government Debt

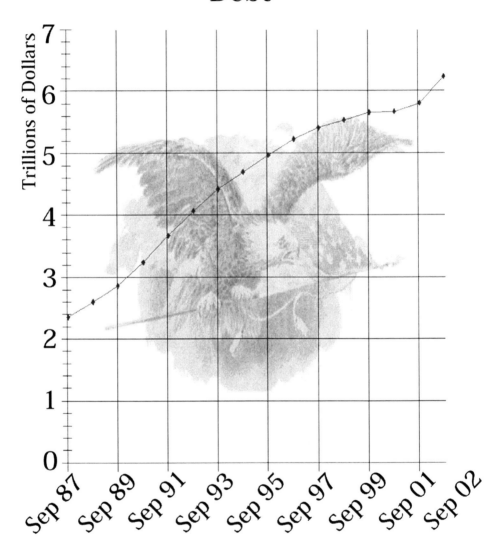

in a static world, yet the BLS apparently thinks we do. This deliberate attempt at deception is prima facie evidence of the Federal Government's need to cook the books. True figures would reveal the fact that the ongoing ruination of the dollar is part and parcel of the Federal Reserve policy. After all, creating "debt money" at will, in massive amounts, is inflation itself. Why don't we simply report the increase in the supply of money? That is really the only meaningful measure of inflation. The utter complicity of the "mainstream press" in continuing this C.P.I. charade is a disservice to the American people. We deserve to be informed as to the growth in the money supply. Otherwise we will keep saving these things called dollars without ever knowing their true value.

Conclusions

Which brings us full circle. What are we to assume going forward. We have reviewed the U.S. Government balance sheet and found it wanting. It is not so much the lack of faith or a pessimistic view of the future, as it is a harsh visible reality. Knowing what we do, let us examine the options open to the economic future of the United States monetary system. First and foremost, you have to stand in awe of this system. A more profitable money machine the world has never known. Just the interest payments on the U.S. debt alone amount to over $300 billion a year. The total Federal spending each year tops $2 trillion. Our total "on the books" public debt exceeds $7 trillion. While off the books liabilities probably push this total over $15 trillion. Mounting demographic challenges suggest further deficits will be the rule of the day. So what is a generation to do? There are basically two options. The case for deflation suggests that the Federal Government will increase borrowing from the public, rein in spending, raise taxes and apply all extra money to paying down the debt. The amount of freshly created money will be curtailed. In a fiat system, as any honestly trained economist will tell you, each time a debt is extinguished, the money representing that debt is withdrawn from circulation. Unless corresponding debt is created, the money supply will shrink. This will result in fewer dollars chasing more goods which means further, that prices will fall. In such a falling price environment the pressures on U.S. business would cause many bankruptcies. Higher taxes would likewise cripple growth and cause more than a slight discomfort to already overburdened Americans. Many authors have made this case for deflation and I must respectfully disagree. It is within this turmoil that the seeds of revolution are sown. Not much profit in that. Keeping the people in the dark concerning their plight, now that is profitable.

The more likely scenario in my view is one of inflation. Using the same metrics provided before, and using identical projections of debt, let us examine the more likely scenario. Firstly, President

Bush has proposed a series of overdue tax cuts.
These will result in a shrinking revenue base.
Furthermore, most Americans feel they are already
overtaxed with nearly half of the typical taxpayer's
cash going to taxes in one form or another.
Additionally, the budget figures suggest a deficit of
$300 billion for FY2003. I believe it is more like
$450 billion. Plus $1.2 trillion in accumulated

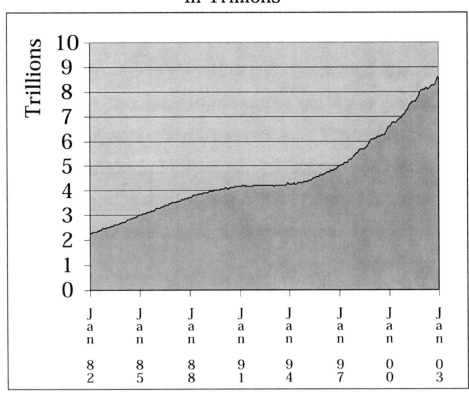

Money Supply M-3 1982-2003
In Trillions

deficits over the next 5 years. Either figure represents a huge amount of public borrowing. Any increases would cause a crowding out of borrowers and cause a rise in interest rates. The danger here is that the international markets will lose patience with the accumulation of U.S. debt and drive the dollar sharply lower. This will reverse the disinflationary effects of the strong dollar and again present the probability of interest rate hikes in the face of recessionary pressures. Right at a time when we will need billions of dollars in available capital.

International bank deposits have increased almost five-fold to over $1 trillion in the last 10 years. International securities issues are also providing stiff competition to U.S. securities issues, recently achieving record volumes. As for reducing spending, I can not think about it without laughing. That is the most ridiculous option of all! Elected officials have been trained. All they know how to do is spend more. Unless they intend to fire the Federal Reserve and keep those earnings, there really is little else to consider. Fully 90 percent of the budget is comprised of entitlements, interest on the debt, or

trust fund repayments. That leaves just 10 cents on
the dollar to cut. I recently had a look at the current
Federal budget. Every politico with aspirations to
another term brags about the projects they bring
home. Senator Ted Stevens of Alaska will get plenty
of votes for the $1,250,000 Congress authorized to
be spent for repairing an Aleutian Pribilof Church.
The $2,500,000 obtained for a pilot training
simulator at the University of Alaska is also quite
popular with the people of Alaska. After all, they
aren't paying for it. Hawaiian Senator Dan Inouye
managed to find $4,500,000 for the construction of
an Observatory facility in Hilo, Hawaii, $2,500,000
for marijuana eradication and $742,000 for the
Native Hawaiian culture and arts program. In New
Mexico, taxpayers will pay $10 million for additions
to the Palace of Governors Museum in Santa Fe.
What do these projects have in common? They are
located in the home States of the key committee
members who decide how to appropriate your tax
dollars. It does not matter if they are voted out.
Whoever takes their place will do exactly the same
thing. You can bet that any politician in the same

bet that any politician in the same position will take
care of their own at the expense of all others. Why
do you think they keep getting reelected? I will bet
you can guess who suggested we spend $200,000 for
the Rep. Maxine Waters Employment Preparation
Center or $150,000 for new office space for Senator
Robert Byrd. But honestly, $4,177,000 to study
shrimp? That one baffles even a cynic like myself.
So you can forget cutting down on spending. What
does that leave? I hope you have guessed by now.
Increase the debt, and let the Federal Reserve
create more money. It is nearly painless. That is
why I believe the only plausible result is inflation.
By creating an extra $5 trillion or so Congress can
provide the best of both worlds. Firstly they will
raise the debt ceiling and issue more bonds. The
GSEs such as FNMA will make unprecedented
bond issues. Secondly the Federal Reserve will
monetize all of this debt and more. All of this
money supply increase will delay the effects of the
problem for at least half a generation. Unless you
have to live on a fixed supply of money, the effects
of inflation will not be too harmful. Higher prices

with rising real estate values will benefit most working Americans. Those who leave their money in bonds or other fixed return assets will bear the brunt of this erosion. Let's face it. They are not the majority in the U.S. The voting public will feel good with all manner of pet project funded. To most politicians this is all that matters and self preservation is an instinct they all possess.

What To Do?

There is an obvious need for clear, comparable and transparent accounting standards at the Federal level. Without accurate accounting, it is impossible to assess the quality of credits, the value of the dollar or the health of the Federal Government. Confusion as to what the Governments' own accounts suggest adds another layer of uncertainty. Both of these problems need to be addressed. Furthermore, there is a great need for more disclosure about the financial activities of the quasi-public sectors, such as The Federal Reserve Banks, FNMA and other GSEs. However, preventing financial crisis, goes beyond having Government reporting. It also requires adequate indicators of any action taken in the banking system. Currency swaps or other manipulations should be taken in the light of day. Dangerous excesses do not instantly appear. They build over time and knowing when the line has been crossed is not easy. Banks should not be allowed to further increase their exposure where there is any form of public guarantee.

Rekindling growth will not be a painless task.
Stimulating the economy through permanent tax
cuts directed at those thought most likely to spend
the extra income is a step in the right direction.
Also it prevents Congress from wasting that money.
The only way real way to stop them is to make
them spend real money. Article 1 Section 8 Clause
10 of the U.S. Constitution has never been repealed:

> *"No State shall make any thing but Gold
> and Silver coin a tender in payment of debt."*

If these folks had to spend real money you could
virtually ignore them. The damage they could do
would be severely limited. They can't just create
gold or silver coins out of thin air. They can still be
represented by electronic entry or paper receipt.
Either way, if Congress has to borrow from an
existing fixed supply of something, prudence would
be guaranteed. Borrowing too much would create a
shortage of money. This uncomfortable shortage of
money would create an incentive for people to vote
the perpetrators out of office. Instant accountability

would be assured. No more putting the problems off on the next generation. Make the hard choices now. Forgive me dear reader, I do not want to give the impression that I am advocating that we rely on some sort of a concerted action such as forcing the Government to follow the Constitution. Honestly, it is a pipe dream. As you can see from the enclosed chart the Federal Reserve has grown the money supply from $2 trillion to almost $9 trillion in a matter of 20 years. The Federal Government has surrendered our gold and our monetary authority long ago. The Federal Reserve took over gold coin distribution and monetary functions in 1913 and by 1933 it was illegal for average Americans to redeem their paper notes for gold coins. Today, it is illegal to convert significant amounts of electronic money into paper money without regulation. Further, the only way to acquire the monetary gold of the United States is through private sale. An auction in the summer of 2002 transferred ownership of the last $20 gold coin issued in 1933. The sum staggered the collecting public. It seems that in a world swimming with electronic dollars, someone was willing to trade 7.5 million of them for 20 dollars gold. A unique piece to be sure but a massive sum indeed. This comes as no surprise to folks who understand real money. The Federal Reserve Bank of New York has amassed the biggest stash of gold coins and bars on the planet. We the people have the biggest pile of debt in the world. What a trade, I suggest it will continue to be business as usual, more electronic money being created that is worth less. Paper money will gradually disappear altogether.

If the U.S. Government is foolish enough to relinquish our gold and silver coin, then it is every citizens duty to seize them. The total face value of all of the U.S. monetary gold issued by the Treasury since 1792 would be spent through the Federal budget in less than 1 hour. I hope you get your share of these gold coins before the value of electronic money is diluted to mere fractions of its current worth.

"Although the gold standard could hardly be portrayed as having produced a period of price tranquility, it was the case that the price level in 1929 was not much different, on net, from what it had been in 1800. But, in the two decades following the abandonment of the gold standard in 1933, the consumer price index in the United States nearly doubled. And, in the four decades after that, prices quintupled. Monetary policy, unleashed from the constraint of domestic gold convertibility, has allowed a persistent over issuance of money. As recently as a decade ago, central bankers, having witnessed more than a half-century of chronic inflation, appeared to confirm that a fiat currency was inherently subject to excess."

Alan Greenspan Speech at the Economic Club of New York on 19th December 2002.

CPSIA information can be obtained at www.ICGtesting.com
Printed in the USA
BVOW040929151111

276098BV00002B/1/P